W9-DEV-685

ASK ISAAC ASIMOV

HOW IS PAPER MADE?

BY ISAAC ASIMOV AND ELIZABETH KAPLAN

Gareth Stevens Publishing
MILWAUKEE

For a free color catalog describing Gareth Stevens' list of high-quality children's books, call 1-800-341-3569 (USA) or 1-800-461-9120 (Canada).

Library of Congress Cataloging-in-Publication Data

Asimov, Isaac. 1920-
    How is paper made? / by Isaac Asimov and Elizabeth Kaplan.
        p.   cm. -- (Ask Isaac Asimov)
    Includes bibliographical references and index.
    Summary: Briefly describes the process involved in making paper and some of the problems associated with the production and use of paper.
    ISBN 0-8368-0803-7
    1. Papermaking—Juvenile literature. [1. Papermaking.]
I. Kaplan, Elizabeth, 1956-   . II. Title. III. Series: Asimov, Isaac, 1920-   Ask Isaac Asimov.
TS1105.5.A85   1993
    676--dc20   92-32551

Edited, designed, and produced by
Gareth Stevens Publishing
1555 North RiverCenter Drive, Suite 201
Milwaukee, Wisconsin 53212, USA

The type of paper used to make this book is called 70# white mountie matte. It is made of 70 percent hardwood fibers and 30 percent softwood fibers. In the chemical process used, called Kraft (or sulfate) pulping, the wood chips are cooked in a chemical solution made of caustic soda and sodium sulfide in order to dissolve the lignin.

At this time, Gareth Stevens, Inc., does not use 100 percent recycled paper, although the paper used in our books does contain about 30 percent recycled fiber. This decision was made after a careful study of current recycling procedures revealed their dubious environmental benefits. We will continue to explore recycling options.

The book designer wishes to thank the models for their helpful cooperation.

Picture Credits
pp. 2-3, © D. Muench/H. Armstrong Roberts; pp. 4-5, © Ken Novak, 1992; pp. 6-7, © E. R. Degginger/Picture Perfect USA; p. 6 (inset), © Mary Evans Picture Library; pp. 8-9, © D. Muench/H. Armstrong Roberts; p. 8 (inset), © Norman Tomalin/Bruce Coleman Limited; pp. 10-11, © John Zoiner; pp. 12-13, © John Zoiner; pp. 14-15, Kurt Carloni/Artisan, 1992; pp.16-17, © John Coster-Mullen/Third Coast Stock Source; pp. 18-19, © Bruce Paton/Panos Pictures; p. 19 (inset), © J. Hartley/Panos Pictures; pp. 20-21, © W. Metzen/H. Armstrong Roberts; pp. 22-23, © D. Muench/H. Armstrong Roberts; p. 24, © D. Muench/H. Armstrong Roberts

Cover photograph, © Chris Wormald/Adams Picture Library: Paper production at Wiggin's Teap Mill in England

Series editor: Valerie Weber
Editors: Barbara J. Behm and Patricia Lantier-Sampon
Series designer: Sabine Beaupré
Book designer: Kristi Ludwig
Picture researcher: Diane Laska

Contents

Words that appear in the glossary are printed in **boldface** type the first time they occur in the text.

Modern-Day Wonders

Pick up your telephone and talk with someone halfway around the world. Press a few buttons on a microwave oven and have a hot dinner in seconds. These are only a few of the many wonders of technology.

One of today's most useful products is paper. Without paper, we'd have no books, newspapers, or letters from friends. Business would grind to a halt. How is paper made? Let's find out.

Paper in the Ancient World

Along the banks of the Nile River, reeds wave gently in the breeze. These simple plants were very important in ancient times. The Egyptians slit the reeds, scraped out the inner fibers, and pressed the fibers together. The result was **papyrus**, a material on which the Egyptians wrote their important records. Papyrus scrolls have survived for more than 4,000 years. Papyrus is thicker than paper. The Chinese people first made paper around A.D. 100.

From Plants Comes Paper

Tear off a corner of a piece of paper and look at the torn edge with a magnifying glass. Notice the tiny fibers that stick out from the paper's edge. These fibers come from plants. They are the main ingredient in paper.

Paper used to be made from scraps of cotton and linen. In the early 1800s, the demand for paper outgrew the scrap cloth supply. People began making paper out of ground-up wood mixed with water. This mixture is called wood pulp.

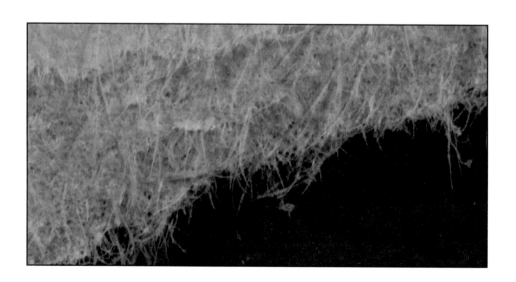

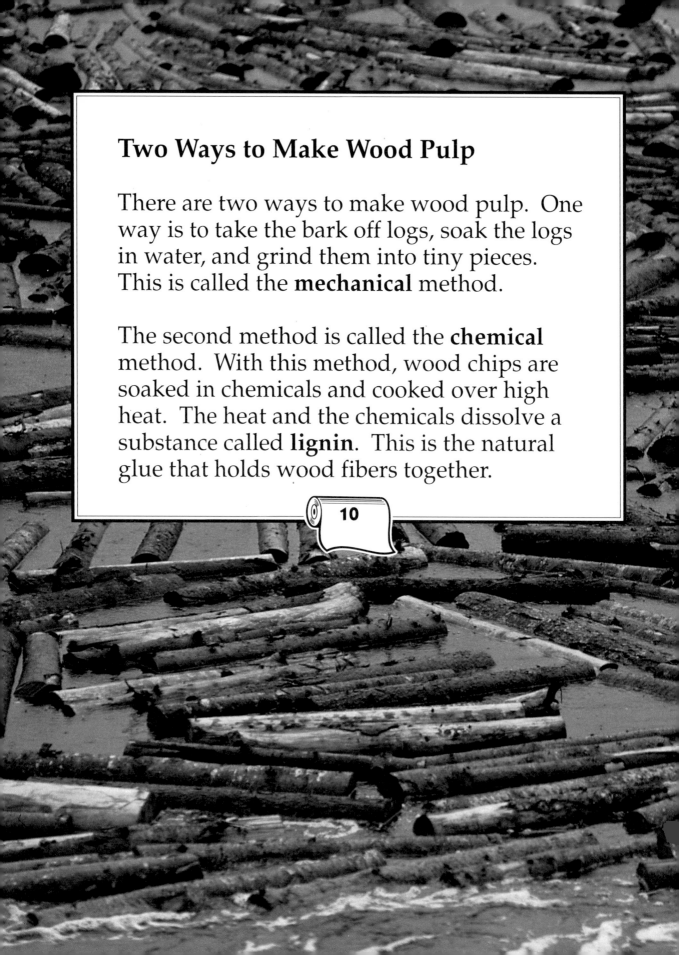

Two Ways to Make Wood Pulp

There are two ways to make wood pulp. One way is to take the bark off logs, soak the logs in water, and grind them into tiny pieces. This is called the **mechanical** method.

The second method is called the **chemical** method. With this method, wood chips are soaked in chemicals and cooked over high heat. The heat and the chemicals dissolve a substance called **lignin**. This is the natural glue that holds wood fibers together.

Preparing Wood Pulp

Wood pulp is washed and pushed through a screen to remove fibers too large for making paper. Then, the smaller fibers are bleached to make them white. Next, different kinds of fibers are blended together. Fibers produced by the mechanical method are used in low-quality paper. Fibers produced by the chemical method are used in high-quality paper. These fibers don't contain lignin, which makes paper yellow with age. Most papers are made of a mixture of the two types of fibers.

13

From Pulp to Paper

Now the wood pulp, which is mostly water, is poured onto a huge, metal screen. Find this screen in the diagram below. The screen moves forward. Rollers press on the screen to remove most of the water. As the wood

14

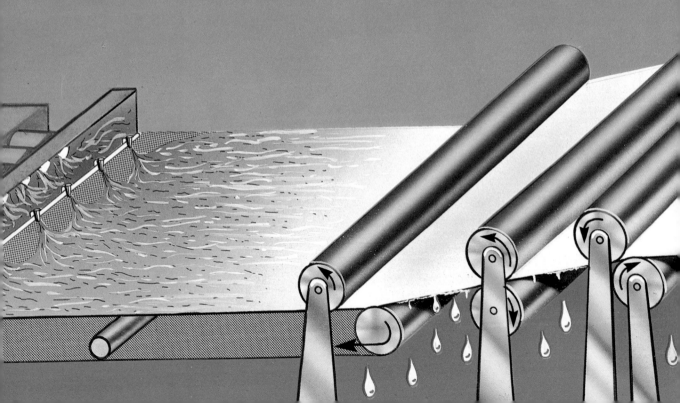

pulp dries, the fibers bond, forming a paper. Iron rollers, called the calendar stack, smooth and polish the paper. Then, the paper is wound onto large rolls. The paper stored on these rolls can be cut into smaller sheets.

15

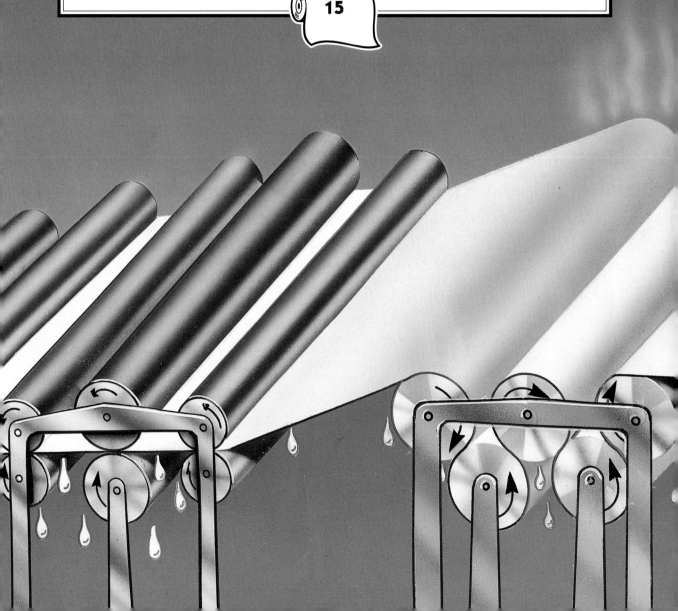

Reusing the Fibers: Recycling Paper

Making wood pulp into paper doesn't destroy the fibers. They can be used again if the paper is **recycled**. Recycling paper involves collecting used paper, sorting it according to color and quality, and cleaning it to remove staples or other non-paper items. Then, the clean, sorted paper is wet down and beaten to loosen the fibers. The recycled fibers can be made into cardboard or newsprint or mixed with wood pulp to make higher-quality paper.

16

Destroying Forests for the Trees

Trees are a mostly **renewable** resource: in theory, if some get cut down, others can be planted. But cutting down trees can be tragic. **Clear-cutting**, removing all the trees in an area, causes the soil to wash away. Trees can't grow back on bare rock. Even if new trees are planted, the forest and its inhabitants may still die off. Sometimes only one type of tree is replanted. So, animals that need other types of trees for food or shelter can no longer live in the forest.

Paper and Water Pollution

Destroying forests isn't the only problem our
hunger for paper causes. Making paper
causes pollution. Most paper companies use
chlorine to bleach wood pulp. Chlorine
mixes with other chemicals that dissolve out

of the wood, forming **dioxins**. Dioxins are
chemicals that can cause cancer. Wastewater
from most paper companies contains these
harmful chemicals. When the water is
dumped into lakes and rivers, dioxins cause
pollution. Fish from the polluted waters are
unsafe to eat.

Solving the Paper Problem

Think of all the ways you use paper. The list is almost endless! But too much of a good thing can cause problems. We can help solve the paper problem by buying unpackaged goods whenever possible, recycling paper, and asking papermakers to stop using chlorine in their papermaking process.

22

More Books to Read

The Amazing Book by Paulette Bourgeois (Addison Wesley)
From Wood to Paper by Ali Mitgutsch (Carolrhoda Books)
Paper, Paper, Everywhere by Gail Gibbons (Harcourt, Brace)
The Secret Life of School Supplies by Vicki Cobb (Lippincott)

Places to Write

Here are some places you can write for more information about papermaking and recycling. Be sure to tell them exactly what you want to know. Give them your full name and address so they can write back to you.

Paper Stock Institute
    c/o The Institute of Scrap
    Recycling Industries
1627 K Street NW
Suite 700
Washington, D.C. 20006

U.S. Forest Service
    Forest Products Laboratory
One Gifford Pinchot Drive
Madison, Wisconsin 53705-2398

American Paper Institute
260 Madison Avenue
New York, New York 10016

Greenpeace Foundation
185 Spadina Avenue, 6th Floor
Toronto, Ontario M5T 2C6

Glossary

chemicals (KEH-mih-kuhls): substances that make up our world. Everything is made up of chemicals. The chemical method of making wood pulp involves using heat and chemicals to break down wood chips.

chlorine (KLOR-een): a chemical that is an active agent in bleaches or whiteners.

clear-cutting: the logging practice of cutting down or removing all the trees in an area of a forest.

dioxin (die-AHK-sihn): a harmful chemical that results when chlorine mixes with materials that dissolve out of wood.

lignin (LIHG-nuhn): a natural glue in wood that holds the fibers together.

mechanical (meh-KAN-ih-kuhl): relating to a machine. The mechanical method of making wood pulp involves grinding logs without bark in water.

papyrus (puh-PIE-ruhs): an ancient Egyptian writing material made from the inner fibers of reeds.

recycle (ree-SIE-kuhl): to reuse a material by cleaning it and recovering the useful elements.

renewable (ree-NOO-ah-buhl): capable of being replaced by natural processes.

Index